90 DAYS *of* RENEWAL

BRUCE DOWNES

90 DAYS OF RENEWAL

ISBN 978-1-7334702-4-7

Published by
Bruce Downes Ministries
PO Box 55750
Phoenix, AZ 85078
Telephone (602) 612-9705
www.BruceDownes.org

90 DAYS *of* RENEWAL

Jim, Molly, Julie, Harry, Scott and Lannette.
Thank You.

Ronan McGinniss, you're a man of integrity,
strength, discipline, hard work and fine character—all
qualities that the Scriptures hold up to all of us
to attain to as we strive to be like Christ.
Thank you for who you are.

DAY 1

Welcome to Day 1 of what will be an amazing 90-day journey! We have called this '90 Days of Renewal' as we genuinely believe that it can have a transformational effect on your life!

To RENEW means to 'restore or begin again.' From time to time it can be invaluable for us to experience renewal in our faith. **We don't have to be without faith to seek renewal.**

Let me explain it this way. Our family car is a fairly common 'run of the mill' vehicle. It's a few years old but is perfectly fine. Most days I am very comfortable with the car and have no real desire to look for anything better.

But I must admit, if I had the opportunity to swap my car for this year's brand-new model, I probably would. To restore my car exactly to the way it was when I first got it would be amazing. Over the years it has become a little worn, suffered a few bumps, and isn't as exciting to drive as it was when it was new.

Our faith can be the same. There might be nothing wrong with our faith. However, over time our faith can feel a little worn, suffer a few bumps and might not feel as exciting as when we were starting out. This means that to 'restore and begin again' is a fantastic opportunity. To renew our faith every now and then can do amazing things for our life.

To get the most out of this journey, there are six things you should do.

THE SIX KEYS TO MAKING '90 DAYS OF RENEWAL' WORK FOR YOU:

1. **COMMIT:** Make the decision RIGHT NOW that you will COMMIT to doing what is asked of you in the next 90 days.

2. **EARLY:** Sit down and read the daily session early in the day rather than putting it off. Being able to think about what you have read during the day will really help your experience. For this reason, it will work best if you only do one session per day.

3. **ACTION:** Don't just read the daily session to increase your knowledge. Take the ACTION that the passage suggests.

4. **JOURNAL:** You will need a blank journal or notebook that you can use to write down answers to the questions for each session, and to use for prayer.

5. **KEEP GOING:** If it so happens that you miss a few days, don't give up! KEEP GOING from the session that you are up to. If it takes you a few days longer to finish the course, it won't be a problem at all.

6. **BE HUNGRY:** Don't just do this because it sounds like a nice idea. BE HUNGRY for a deeper faith and a deeper relationship with Jesus. Even if you don't know what this really means, BE HUNGRY for something better.

Now that you have some idea of what to expect, we will dive straight into it tomorrow. The normal daily sessions won't be as long as this session... it will be short enough for you to read and reflect on the moment you see it.

I look forward to doing this journey with you.

God Bless,

Bruce Downes
The Catholic Guy

DAY 2

There are some examples in the scriptures of people who experience renewal in a quick and immediate way, even in an instant. However, for most of us renewal occurs over time. Renewal often occurs in a special location or place. Some people go away to retreat centres with lovely gardens, others spend time in a cathedral or church.

In the busyness of everyday life, it is often difficult to go to these places each and every day. Therefore, it can be very beneficial to find your own place that you can sit for a few minutes each day of this renewal journey. For me it's a particular lounge chair in the sitting room of our house. For others it might be a park bench that they walk past every day, or a seat on the back veranda.

I call this my 'Prayer Place.' It helps me to shut out the world as I ask God for renewal each day. To help you during these '90 Days of Renewal' I encourage you to find your own prayer place.

 TODAY'S QUESTION:
What place can you allocate as your daily 'prayer place?'

 TODAY'S ACTION:
Sit in this prayer place for just 5 minutes and reflect on the many things in your busy life that you can leave behind every time to sit in this place.

DAY 3

To experience renewal in our faith we need to overhaul the daily habits and practices of our life. As we go through life we develop many habits, some of which are good and some which may be detrimental to our wellbeing.

By the end of '90 Days of Renewal' you will have developed a number of brand new habits that will strengthen your faith and improve your life.

Today we want you to think about your current regular habits, both good and bad. They may have nothing to do with faith and that's ok. Positive habits could include things like eating a piece of fruit each morning, kissing your spouse when you return home from work and always reading a few pages of a book before you go to sleep.

Negative habits could include putting three sugars in your coffee, making negative comments or spending money on magazines that you know are a waste of your time.

 TODAY'S QUESTION:
What are your POSITIVE habits and NEGATIVE habits?

 TODAY'S ACTION:
Write down a list of these POSITIVE and NEGATIVE habits. *(Try and do this whilst sitting in your PRAYER PLACE)*

DAY 4

Yesterday we looked at the positive and negative habits that you currently have in your life. It goes without saying that you should begin removing the negative habits from your daily life. With God's help this is definitely possible, and we will look more at this later.

Over the remainder of this 90-day journey we will look at numerous other daily habits that you can develop to help you in your faith. We won't look at 90 of them, don't worry! That would be overkill!

One of the most important daily actions of a Christian person is to pray. Prayer takes many, many forms. Again, we will look at numerous ways of praying as we progress.

Today, let's keep it simple. Reflect on the question below and then complete the action. It will work best if you do this whilst sitting in your prayer place.

TODAY'S QUESTION:
What would you say to Jesus if you could write Him a letter and pop it in the mail?

TODAY'S ACTION:
Open to a blank page, start by writing 'Dear Jesus' at the top and then write. Don't over think it. Write down whatever comes to mind; questions, fears, joys, feelings. Try and make this last for a full five minutes.

DAY 5

Yesterday's action (DAY 4) is one action that you can't skip, as it will make the rest of this course seem strange. So if you need to, look back at yesterday's session and go back through it.

Now to today...

Reflect on how yesterday's letter to God felt to write. For some people it will have been free-flowing and also very rewarding. For others it would have been extremely difficult and very uncomfortable. I want to encourage you to do the same thing every single day! Even if it's difficult. Start with just five minutes per day.

When you do this it's far more than just a nice exercise. It is genuine prayer! It might not feel like other prayer experiences you have had, but it most definitely is prayer. In fact, pouring out your daily thoughts to God is one of the most authentic prayers that you can pray.

Before we move on to other kinds of habits that bring renewal, you really want to become more comfortable with praying daily.

TODAY'S ACTION:

Open to another blank page and write another letter to God. Seeing as you wrote one yesterday, today's one might focus more on today's thoughts, struggles and joys. Try again to make this last a full five minutes.

DAY 6

A s you are well aware, the daily habit that we are currently working on is the habit of daily prayer.

There is an important aspect to prayer that we now need to introduce. Prayer is not just about talking to God. **Prayer is also about listening to God.** Every day I write out my prayers just like I have encouraged you to do the past few days. But I also spend some time listening to God.

I am not talking about things like listening for audible voices or looking for images in the sky. There are a few people who have experienced this throughout history, but most people who experience this need to speak with a psychologist straight away!

Three ways we can listen for what God might be saying to us whilst we pray:

1. Reflect on the things that happened in the past day. Did anything take you by surprise and could this be God speaking to you through these circumstances?

2. Reflect on the thoughts, feelings and convictions that have gone through your head in the past day. Could this be God speaking to you through your conscience?

3. Have you heard any wise words, especially from people you know that have a great faith?

These three ways are enough for now. We will build on this down the track.

TODAY'S QUESTION:
What might God be saying to you today?

TODAY'S ACTION:
When you sit with your journal today, start as you have by sharing your thoughts with God. Then, think through these THREE WAYS above and write down things that come to you. This could well be God speaking to you.

DAY 7

Yesterday I encouraged you to expand the scope of your daily prayer time to include some reflection on what God might be saying to you. We looked at three ways to listen to God during this time.

There is one extremely valuable and reliable way of listening to God that we will introduce right now. This is of course listening to God through reading **sacred scripture**. The Bible is not just a historical book about other people's experiences. It really does contain the words that God wants to speak to you and me today.

We can of course read the Bible to gain knowledge about Jesus, faith and Christian beliefs. However, we can also read it to gain knowledge about how the creator of the universe wants us to live our lives, and how we should act or respond to almost any situation or circumstance.

I include the reading of scripture in my prayer time every day, and I would like to encourage you to do the same. If you reflect on it deeply, you will indeed be listening to God.

TODAY'S ACTION 1:

Get a Bible that you can use each day during your prayer time. All versions are of course God's word. The Jerusalem Bible is the version used for the Mass readings, and the NRSV is a common Catholic study bible.

TODAY'S ACTION 2:

During your prayer time read Matthew 5:1-11. This is a famous passage called 'The Beatitudes.' As you read through it (maybe even a few times) reflect on what God might be saying to you through the words of this text and write these thoughts down.

DAY 8

Congratulations! You have made your way through the first week of '90 Days of Renewal.' The most important thing that we have looked at so far is developing the habit of daily prayer.

I cannot stress this enough. Since I was first taught how to pray daily it has revolutionised my faith and my life.

The way I have spent my prayer time each day has gradually changed and developed over the years, but **a few key things have always remained central to my prayer time.** These are:

Praying in a consistent place

Writing out my prayers in a journal

Writing out what I believe God is saying to me

Reading and reflecting on scripture

To get the most out of prayer it is better to allocate quality time to it. I also recommend allocating a QUANTITY of time to it. So far I have suggested you pray for five minutes each day. I know some people who pray for many hours a day but this is not for everyone. I recommend that you work up to the point where you will pray for a minimum of fifteen minutes each day.

TODAY'S QUESTION:
Have you prayed for at least five minutes every day this week?

TODAY'S ACTION:

Extend your prayer time to ten minutes (every day for the next week). When doing the scripture reading, read the section that follows on from The Beatitudes. This will be Matthew 5:13-16. Every section under a new heading is called a 'pericope.' Each day this week read the next pericope that follows in the book of Matthew.

DAY 9

We have focussed so far on talking and listening to God through our own personal prayer time. Hopefully you are already experiencing a sense of renewal in your faith!

It is important also to appreciate that God also speaks to us at other times and in other ways.

One of the ways God speaks to us is through spiritual friends and mentors.

I am fortunate to have known many people in my life that have spoken defining words to me. On many occasions their words have been so significant that I had no doubt that they were in fact speaking God's will to me.

TODAY'S QUESTION:
Who is a person in your life that God might be using to speak to you?

TODAY'S ACTION:
Change the way that you think about people in your life. Begin to think of the person that you know as the living image of God the Father, and listen to their words as if it was in fact the physical person of Jesus.

Remember also to pray for ten minutes each day, including the reading of a passage of scripture.

DAY 10

T oday we are going to introduce a new habit. What I will share with you today will have an amazing effect on the renewal of your faith if you let it.

This daily habit is called an **EXAMINATION OF CONSCIENCE.** You may already be familiar with it, but by implementing this at a deeper level, the way you live your life can genuinely be transformed.

An examination of conscience is a prayerful self reflection on our words and actions in the light of the Gospel. It allows us to determine how we may have fallen short on living the way God asks us to.

To make it easier for you, some of these questions might help you examine your conscience:

- Which of my words should I not have spoken today?

- Which of my actions were harmful to others today?

- Which of my actions were harmful to myself today?

- What decisions did I make today that I shouldn't have made?

- What did I not do today that I should have done?

TODAY'S ACTION:

Take two minutes to ask yourself these questions above. Try and do so in a prayerful manner. Maybe do this as part of your prayer time, or maybe just as you put your head on the pillow tonight.

DAY 11

Yesterday we looked at beginning to implement the daily habit of the examination of conscience. This practice is too valuable to have just mentioned it in yesterday's session and to leave it there. Allow me to give you some extra thoughts and tips as to how you can gain even more and more from it each day.

The examination of conscience is more than just reflecting on the day. It is about reminding ourselves of the way that a Christian is called to live and being aware of ways we might be off track from this plan.

To do this effectively we need to make sure that we have a clear understanding of the way a Christian is supposed to live. It's not easy to summarise it and write it down here for you, so you will need to get an understanding of this yourself.

A good place for us to start is developing a conviction and understanding of the Ten Commandments.

TODAY'S ACTION:
Read the Ten Commandments (found in the book of Exodus 20:1-17). After you read, then reflect on each of them and examine your own conscience to see if God reveals things to you that you need to improve.

DAY 12

How is '90 Days of Renewal' going for you so far? Are you practising the new daily habits of daily prayer, scripture reading and examination of conscience?

Remember that this is a 90-day journey. I am deliberately not telling you everything I know right at the beginning. Developing intimacy with Jesus is not about having lots and lots of knowledge and new information thrown upon you all at once.

Think of it like studying geometry or chemistry. I could throw a textbook on your desk and then hope that by the next day you are fully qualified. You know as well as I do that this wouldn't work for anyone. It takes fifteen or twenty years of formal education before someone can be qualified in these areas and even then, they will still continually learn whilst working professionally.

We also know that the breadth and complexity of God is far larger than geometry or chemistry. It will take a lifetime to even try and master the things of faith... so if we are going to try and achieve a real sense of renewal in 90 days we better not go too fast!

 TODAY'S QUESTION:
Are you spending ten minutes every day in prayer? Have you done this yet today?

TODAY'S ACTION:

Ensure that you spend your ten minutes of daily prayer where you talk to God, listen to God, read and reflect on scripture and examine your conscience.

DAY 13

This 90-day season is not meant to be a course on the A-Z of Christian beliefs, so we are not going to get the opportunity to describe all components of every aspect in detail.

Some days when life is busy, I pray a different way and I call it the stress prayer. This should not be the norm, but it is necessary from time to time. If you know that you are not going to pray on a given day due to your life circumstances, then when you wake in the morning say to God,

> *"Lord, I love You and I ask You to be with me through this busy day. Watch over me, keep my family and me safe and may the decisions I make today reflect my commitment to You."*

Stress prayer is a small amount of prayer and just as you can't live on a diet forever, it sometimes is necessary for a time.

TODAY'S QUESTION:
Are there things in your life that are making you feel stressed and busy and distracted as you pray?

TODAY'S ACTION:
In your journal make a list of things that are currently creating busyness or stress in your life. Ask God to help you to let them go and be with you in this season.

DAY 14

You are now two weeks into '90 Days of Renewal.' Well done! We have looked at the new habits of:

- Daily prayer

- Scripture reading

- Examination of conscience

About a week ago I encouraged you to aim to spend ten minutes each day in personal prayer. **Now I would like to challenge you to spend fifteen minutes per day in prayer.** Don't worry, next week I am not going to up it by another five minutes and then continually increase it again and again. I personally encourage people to pray for at least fifteen minutes every day. If others (or God) encourage you to spend longer praying then naturally that's a good thing.

Remember that praying in a consistent place and writing out my prayers has been invaluable to me. If you think that jumping from ten to fifteen minutes each day will be tough, then these two things might also be a big help to you.

TODAY'S ACTION:
Increase your daily prayer time to fifteen minutes, and continue this each and every day.

DAY 15

M y hope and prayer is that you were able to extend your personal prayer time yesterday to fifteen minutes and that you were able to sense God's presence with you.

In the next section of this 90-day course we are going to do something a little different. For the next few weeks I am not going to be giving you any more NEW HABITS to do. This is because I want you to focus on the habits we have already spoken about, dedicating fifteen minutes of the day to them.

This next section will give you things to focus on during your daily prayer time and also things to think about in regards to your daily actions.

Back on Day 7 we started reading the Bible by reading 'The Beatitudes' found in Matthew 5. A few days later we started the discipline of examining our conscience. To do this we reflected on the Ten Commandments, however, we can also reflect on each of The Beatitudes to do the same.

For the next ten days we will look at a different one of The Beatitudes. We will start today with the first one.

> *"God blesses those who realise their need for him, for the Kingdom of Heaven is given to them."*

> Matthew 5:3 (NLT)

As we grow up in life, we are preparing to be able to do things for ourselves. We are taught to read, to understand, to work, to earn money and to live independently. However, at some stage we will realise that there are some things in life that we can't do, and many that we find difficult to do.

Instead of 'giving up' we can ask God, and depend on God, to walk with us in this unknown.

TODAY'S QUESTION:

What things in your life are a reminder to you that you really do need God in your life?

TODAY'S ACTION:

During your prayer time, write a list of things that come to mind when you answer the above question. When doing your 'examination of conscience' think of times throughout the past day that you may not have turned to God, and instead relied only on your own strength or ability.

DAY 16

Y ou will remember from yesterday that we are looking at one of 'The Beatitudes' each day and using these to help us in our daily thoughts and actions, as well as our examination of conscience.

> *"God blesses those who mourn, for they will be comforted."*

> Matthew 5:4 (NLT)

This Beatitude is an interesting one. I say this because for most people we don't feel the need to genuinely 'mourn' each day, and nor do we need to. But, as one of the Beatitudes it is an important part of our overall approach to our faith and cannot be ignored.

TODAY'S QUESTION:
Has there been a time in your life when something terrible has happened? It could be the death of a loved one, a tough family situation, the loss of something important or the end of a hope or dream.

How did you respond to this? Did you 'mourn' or did you bottle it up? Did you express emotion or did you try and hide it away? God's way is that we should mourn. Even if it makes us feel weak, it is a reminder to us that God can (and does) provide strength and comfort.

TODAY'S ACTION:

During your prayer time, write a list of the occasions that come to mind when you answer the above question. If you need to shed a tear, or express emotion to God, know that this is God's will, and ask for His comfort.

DAY 17

Today's Beatitude is:

> *"God blesses those who are gentle and lowly, for the whole earth will belong to them."*

Matthew 5:5 (NLT)

This should not be misunderstood as being a person of weakness. Gentleness is something far different and in fact gives great strength and power to your life. Gentleness means that others find you approachable. It means that others don't fear you and are willing to seek you out.

Lowly doesn't mean that you are defeated. Lowly means that others feel that you value them and that you don't act like you are more important than they are.

'Gentle and lowly' shouldn't be confused with 'quietness.' I can recall many people who are very quiet in nature, but when approached are not gentle or lowly in their manner or response.

 TODAY'S QUESTION:
Do you consider yourself as a person who is gentle and lowly?

TODAY'S ACTION:

Take a real risk and ask one of the mature people in your life how they would rate your gentleness? This may give you something to work on. It's also a question you can ask yourself during your daily examination of conscience.

DAY 18

Today's Beatitude is:

"God blesses those who hunger and thirst for justice, for they will be satisfied."

Matthew 5:6 (NLT)

There are many amazing organisations engaging with the issues of social justice. However, this doesn't mean that we shouldn't be developing our own convictions about social justice or making our own personal contribution.

How often do we put a few coins in a tin for a special appeal? The big question is... does A FEW COINS demonstrate HUNGER AND THIRST FOR JUSTICE? Only you can answer this.

As we look at Jesus' words, we realise that it's not the coins that are important, like we often think it is. It's developing a HUNGER AND THIRST! This needs to be done before we even give a cent, and it will determine whether we should give ten cents or ten thousand dollars.

TODAY'S QUESTION:
Are you hungry and thirsty for justice? Do your actions toward those suffering from injustice show that you are?

35

TODAY'S ACTION:

Consider which issue of injustice really tugs at your heart and find a way to make a contribution towards it. It may be a contribution of money, goods, your time, and also your prayer.

DAY 19

Today's Beatitude is:

"God blesses those who are merciful, for they will be shown mercy."

Matthew 5:7 (NLT)

Mercy is not exactly the same as social injustice. It is linked, but it's not the same. Mercy is something we should show to everyone in our world, including those who are not a victim of injustice. It is something we should demonstrate to our family, friends, colleagues and neighbours.

Mercy is the showing of compassion or kindness to someone, even if they have done wrong, are in a position of weakness, or are undeserving.

Thank goodness for mercy! This is what God shows to us each and every day.

TODAY'S QUESTION:
Are you a person of mercy? How have you shown mercy today, or recently?

TODAY'S ACTION:
When you do an examination of conscience today, think through recent opportunities you had to show mercy to others, and consider how you responded.

(Remember to keep up your daily disciplines of prayer, scripture reading and examination of conscience, even if the daily session doesn't specifically remind you to.)

DAY 20

Today's Beatitude is:

"God blesses those whose hearts are pure, for they will see God."

Matthew 5:8 (NLT)

What are your motivations for the things you do? They may not be evil, but are they pure? Australians are excellent at telling whether someone is genuinely telling the truth or not. It's part of our culture. When our political leaders go on TV and make a statement, we don't automatically believe them (as happens in some cultures). We often question their motives and easily recognise when they don't really believe the things that come from their own mouths.

Integrity is such an important characteristic for a Christian person. When you serve someone is it to make yourself look good or because you really care? When you spend time with someone is it out of love or a sense of duty?

It may look the same on the outside, but as this Beatitude says, if our heart is pure then we will see God.

It's crazy to think that we might be doing good things, but if we are doing them for the wrong reason then it will prevent us from seeing God. This might be harsh to accept, but it's God's way.

TODAY'S QUESTION AND ACTION:

During your prayer time today make a list of all of the things you have done with your time and money in the past few days. Then go through the list one by one and prayerfully ask yourself the question: 'why did I do this? Were my intentions totally pure?'

DAY 21

T oday's Beatitude is:

> *"God blesses those who work for peace, for they will be called the children of God."*

Matthew 5:9 (NLT)

To live in peace is such a valuable characteristic of a society. A country where peace is present is a wonderful place to live. But this doesn't take place automatically. It takes forgiveness, understanding, humility and the defence of the weak.

If peace is important to a society then it is also important to our own families, workplaces and communities.

Are the places you spend your time peaceful places? Have you had a peaceful day today? Have others around you had a peaceful day today?

This Beatitude tells us that we shouldn't just enjoy peace, we should WORK for it. We must be intentional and deliberate.

TODAY'S QUESTION AND ACTION:
When doing your examination of conscience today, ask yourself the question 'in what circumstances today did I put my own preferences or comfort aside so that peace might prevail? Were there situations where I could have, but perhaps didn't?'

DAY 22

T oday's Beatitude is:

"God blesses those who are persecuted for doing right, for the Kingdom of Heaven is theirs."

Matthew 5:10 (NLT)

This Beatitude is a strange one. I say this because 'persecution' is not something that we should actively seek out. In fact, if we go out with the intention of creating situations of persecution, we are probably not living out the previous Beatitude and 'working for peace.'

So what does this Beatitude mean? **It means that if you live for God you will occasionally (and maybe even often) be persecuted.**

I believe that we can take two things away from this:

When we suffer the hardships of persecution we can delight in the knowledge that God will bless us with the Kingdom of Heaven.

If we live for God, we may occasionally be persecuted. If I haven't been persecuted lately then MAYBE I am not living out my faith to the extent that I should? It's something to think about anyway.

TODAY'S QUESTION:
Have I been persecuted because of my faith? Will I be ready for this when it occurs, so that I can stand firm?

TODAY'S ACTION:

During your prayer time today, list all of the groups of people that exist in your life. This may include family, different friendship groups, colleagues and acquaintances. Reflect on whether you are displaying that you 'live for God' to each of these groups.

DAY 23

Yesterday we looked at the last Beatitude from Matthew 5.
Let's do a little summary of what we have covered since we
started '90 Days of Renewal.'

We have looked at the daily disciplines of:

- Daily prayer

- Scripture reading

- Examination of conscience (and using the Ten
  Commandments and The Beatitudes to do this)

Hopefully you can see how everything fits together.

Focusing on the Beatitudes alone can give you enough to fill your
daily fifteen minute prayer time. Focusing on only the Beatitudes in
your daily actions will give you enough things for you to make a big
difference in your world.

In tomorrow's session we will launch into another list of important
things, but for now it's important that you cement everything that
has been covered so far.

TODAY'S QUESTION AND ACTION:
In your personal prayer time answer the following
questions:

Have I spent my designated time in prayer for all of the past twenty two days?

What are the things that are distracting me from praying every day?

The thing I am finding most beneficial about having a daily prayer time is...

My greatest desire for the rest of this course is...

DAY 24

In the sessions over the next six days I am going to cover six things that I have been teaching at our live events for many years. You might discover that you know what they are. Bear in mind that this 90 days is not about information, it is about providing an opportunity for renewal.

I am going to talk about something unrelated to your daily fifteen minute prayer time, but I can't encourage you enough to continually focus on your daily prayer time even when the session reading doesn't make reference to it.

I am going to talk about: **How to Walk Daily With God.** In essence, it is about how to walk closely with God during the times that you are not sitting down and praying.

The first thing we can do to walk daily with God is: **daily surrender**

Strangely enough, this also aligns with the first of the Beatitudes:

> *"God blesses those who realise their need for him, for the Kingdom of Heaven is given to them."*

> Matthew 5:3 (NLT)

Every day we should admit our dependence on God. Every day we should give our cares, concerns and fears over to God and be conscious of Him as we tackle these things throughout the day.

It is like developing a relationship with a person. If you say 'I love you' just once then over time the relationship will weaken. By reminding them of your love daily, the relationship will strengthen. This is how we can approach our relationship with God.

TODAY'S ACTION:
Take a moment to stop and surrender to God. Maybe write a reminder somewhere so that you can remember to do this tomorrow, and every day!

DAY 25

The second thing we can do to walk daily with God is: **make God your first thought and last thought.**

If we want to be aware of God's presence throughout the whole day, it makes sense that we begin our day by **making God our first thought.** I try and make an effort to briefly acknowledge God even before I turn my alarm off in the morning. I know of another man who gets out of his bed by deliberately falling onto his knees so that he can briefly bow before God and ask God to be with him during the coming day.

The first thought can be as simple as: "God, I want to do this day with You" or "thank You for this day, Lord."

Similarly, **making God our last thought can make a big difference.** As you turn out the light each night and put your head on the pillow, share a few words with God. You may wish to thank God for the blessings of the day or seek His continued presence in the struggles... or both!

 TODAY'S ACTION:
As you go to bed tonight, practise 'last thought' and when you wake in the morning practise 'first thought.'

DAY 26

The third thing we can do to walk daily with God is: **have constant conversation with God.**

This discipline involves us talking to God continually throughout the day. We can easily do this in our head, and on some occasions it can be done out loud. Every time you have to make a decision, ask God for a little guidance. Every time something good happens, tell God. Every time you face a difficulty, tell God.

We don't do this to tell God things that He doesn't know, we do it to become more aware of God's presence ourselves. As we become more aware that God is so close to us, it will begin to change our words, actions and decisions to be more like Jesus.

Go on, be brave, it may be many years since you had an imaginary friend! This time, your imaginary friend is invisible, but not imaginary!

TODAY'S ACTION:
Write a reminder on your hand or in a place that you look constantly throughout the day. Whenever you see the reminder, share your current thought with God.

DAY 27

The fourth thing we can do to walk daily with God is: **have an expectation of experiencing God.**

As you mature in your Christian journey you will become very good at doing the right Christian things.

Have you ever said your prayers out of habit? Don't get me wrong, it's a good habit, but it's supposed to be so much more than a habit!

It's important that as you go about your day that you actually expect to experience God. If you expect things, you will begin to notice them. When you notice them, it will be a great encouragement to your faith.

When you pray, God may actually speak to you! When you ask, God may actually provide for you, when you receive communion, Jesus will actually transform you.

TODAY'S QUESTION:
Do you genuinely expect that you will somehow experience God today?

TODAY'S ACTION:
Change your thinking and develop an awareness that at any moment, you might have a real and powerful experience of God.

DAY 28

The fifth thing we can do to walk daily with God is: **allow transformation to take place.**

One of the things many people find hard is CHANGE. If we find it hard when things change around us, we will definitely find it hard to CHANGE OURSELVES. However, to walk deeper with God it will require an amount of change on our part.

This discipline involves us allowing God to continually change us, and not being set in our ways such that it prevents this. We should be open to the fact that God can and will transform us, again and again.

The Bible says:

> "*Lord, you are our Father. We are the clay and you are the potter. We are all formed by your hand.*"
>
> Isaiah 64:8 (NLT)

Every day we should allow God to mould as if we were clay. We should be expectant that by the end of the day we may in fact be a transformed person because of having walked closer with God.

TODAY'S QUESTION:
Will you allow God to transform you today, if He chooses to?

TODAY'S ACTION:

Reflect on the little things that happen today and question whether God is trying to encourage some kind of change in you through these things.

DAY 29

The sixth thing we can do to walk daily with God is: **receive constant input.**

The expanses of God's creation are endless. In the same way, what we can know about God is endless. Yet again, our Christian journey on earth is an endless journey!

I know many people who are relying on their 'primary or grade school' understanding of God to make their adult decisions about faith. The people I know who walk deeply with God in their adult lives are the people who seek constant spiritual input. They don't rely on past knowledge alone. I can honestly say that it is the constant input I have sought out that has made me the person I am today. I get any kind of input that I can. I buy lots of recorded talks, I read spiritual books, I listen to a lot of Christian music, I go to conferences and retreats, and I seek the wisdom of others I know.

Constant input is the reason we produce most of what we do in The Catholic Guy ministry. Constant input is the very reason we have written this 90-day course.

It is so important to make time to constantly input into yourself. Anything that doesn't grow or is neglected eventually dies. I don't know about you, but I never want my faith to die.

TODAY'S QUESTION:

Have you been inputting enough spiritual content into your life recently?

TODAY'S ACTION:

If you have skipped some of the session readings and actions in the course so far, go back and do the ones you have missed. If you are finding that doing these daily sessions is not enough, then start reading a spiritual book to give you additional input whilst '90 Days of Renewal' continues.

DAY 30

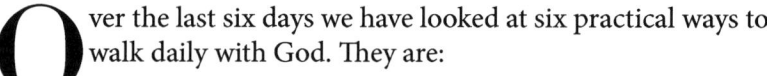

Over the last six days we have looked at six practical ways to walk daily with God. They are:

1. **Daily surrender**

2. **Make God your first thought and last thought**

3. **Have constant conversation with God**

4. **Have an expectation of experiencing God**

5. **Allow transformation to take place**

6. **Receive constant input**

Before moving on to the next things that this course will teach, it is important that you cement these things. In reality it will take many years to properly cement these things, but we will do what we can for now.

I strongly suggest that you write them down and put them in a place where you will see them and be constantly reminded to practice them. I know some people who have them on the dashboard of their car and others who have them on their desk in their workplace.

 TODAY'S QUESTION:
Which of these six things have you done this week?
Which have you found most difficult?

TODAY'S ACTION:
Write these six things in a place you will see them and choose one.

DAY 31

The premise of personal prayer is that it is a relationship that needs to be maintained and deepened during our whole life. Praying to God should be a daily intention and not a haphazard event.

Rosemary and I built our relationship by spending time together but there are days when we simply cannot spend time together. Life is just too busy and full.

I used to be very hesitant about missing prayer because once you say it's ok to miss, it's as if permission is given to miss whenever it gets a little hard.

I have come to learn, however, that it is not the record of never missing that counts but the attitude of my heart and the love I have for God that counts the most.

There are two types of missing out on daily prayer. Firstly, there are those busy periods in life where life is so full and pressured. Secondly, there are those days when I just say, "No, I am not going to pray," which is just lack of discipline to pray.

When I miss due to my slackness, I simply ask God to forgive me. In my prayer journal I may write exactly that.

 TODAY'S QUESTION:
What reasons do you have for missing your daily prayer time?

TODAY'S ACTION:
Write in your journal asking God for forgiveness, strength and resolve for those days.

DAY 32

W ow. It's Day 32 and we are more than a third of the way through '90 Days of Renewal.' Many behavioural experts say that it takes about a month of doing something to create a new habit. Is daily prayer now becoming a habit? You will know that it is when you tend to naturally drift to it rather than have to schedule it or be reminded. If it takes longer than a month don't worry, we have fifty eight more days in this course.

The Gifts of the Holy Spirit have been given to you by God to help you in your everyday life. They are:

- Wisdom

- Understanding

- Right Judgment

- Courage

- Knowledge

- Reverence

- Wonder and Awe

Over the next seven days we will look at each of these seven gifts separately, and look at ways that you can integrate them into your daily life.

TODAY'S QUESTION:

Without looking at the list above, would you have been able to list the seven gifts of the Holy Spirit?

TODAY'S ACTION:

In your personal prayer time, reflect on whether you have consciously decided to implement any of these gifts into your life before? *(Don't despair if you haven't. God is very likely to have activated these gifts in you without you even knowing it.)*

DAY 33

Today we begin looking at the first of the seven Gifts of the Holy Spirit. This is a time to further release these gifts that God has given us into our everyday life.

The first Gift of the Holy Spirit is: **Wisdom.**

Wisdom is one of the hardest things to define, but it's easy to recognise when we see it. Wisdom is impossible to gain from reading a book and it can't be bought with money.... nor can it be taught in a 90-day course!

Thank goodness wisdom is given to us by God! If not for this, it would be hard to get!

The best way to think about wisdom is to reflect on the people you know who display wisdom. It is often present in older people, but it doesn't have to be older people alone. **Wisdom is normally put in action when we see people make decisions or give advice that applies past learning into current situations.**

Do you display wisdom? Do people come to you for advice? Do you reflect on experiences and use your reflection to help you and others in the future?

On the other hand, are you often making the same mistake again and again?

TODAY'S QUESTION:

Who is someone you know that you consider a 'wise person?' What makes them wise?

TODAY'S ACTION:

The gift of wisdom has been given to you if you are baptised. Today, be AWARE that you have this gift, keep it on your mind all day, and reflect on how this changes your day and the day of people around you.

DAY 34

The second Gift of the Holy Spirit is: **Understanding**.

I wish this meant that I knew everything about everything! Unfortunately it doesn't! However, God has gifted us with the intellect and ability to seek out answers to the things relevant to our lives.

Are you frustrated by some things in your world such that you have no understanding of why they are 'the way they are?'

Through the gift of understanding the Holy Spirit is able to give you a peacefulness and appreciation of these situations, even if you don't understand all of the intricacies. God wants to give me understanding of how to be a parent, but God may not want for me to know exactly how the ozone layer works.

I am often reminded that if I knew EVERYTHING, that would make me equal to God! I definitely don't want that responsibility. If you have seen the movie *Bruce Almighty* you will see the havoc that will likely occur if a human became God!

TODAY'S QUESTION AND ACTION:
In your personal prayer time make a list of anything in your world in which you don't understand why the situation is the way it is. After making the list prayerfully reflect on each and see if God reveals to you a sense of peace regarding any of these things. It may take many months or years for you to get a full understanding of some things.

DAY 35

The third Gift of the Holy Spirit is: **Right Judgment**.

We talked about something similar two days ago when we looked at the gift of WISDOM. Wisdom definitely leads to using the gift of RIGHT JUDGMENT.

Cardinal Joseph Cardijn developed a simple and effective method of taking action in our life based on the three words: SEE, JUDGE, ACT. It has become well known and beneficial for millions of people worldwide.

When you see anything it will likely result in action of some kind.

- When you see a cat on the road as you drive, it will elicit some kind of action

- When you see a person in need, it will elicit some kind of action

- When you see someone put a meal on the table, it will elicit some kind of action

The action you take will be a result of your JUDGMENT. Your judgment can be informed principally by the Ten Commandments, but also The Beatitudes and your broader understanding of the scriptures and the life of Jesus.

TODAY'S QUESTION:

When is the last time you considered 'God's perspective' when you made a decision?

TODAY'S ACTION:

As you approach every decision today, consciously incorporate the SEE, JUDGE, ACT method into your decision making.

DAY 36

The fourth Gift of the Holy Spirit is: **Courage**.

I was once in a seminar session where a priest was answering general questions posed to him by the group. One person asked the priest "why does God give some people an easy life and other people a difficult life?" The priest responded by saying "that's an excellent question. In fact I might get everyone who has always had an easy life to raise their hand please." As you can imagine, not a single person raised their hand.

The priest continued and explained that the journey of life for every person has the potential for times of joy and also for times of suffering. Without the gift of courage, we might indeed experience more periods of suffering.

When we ask God to activate the gift of courage, we open ourselves up to an amazing possibility. It doesn't always 'switch on' straight away, but through God's strength we all have the ability to use courage to survive and sometimes avoid periods of difficulty.

 TODAY'S QUESTION:
Has there been a time in your life that you have experienced hardship? When was this?

TODAY'S ACTION:

As you face a situation of hardship today, even if it's only a little thing, stop and pray to God for courage. It might not change the situation, but it will change the way it affects you!

DAY 37

The fifth Gift of the Holy Spirit is: **Knowledge**.

The complexity of the human body is amazing. The extensiveness of the brain alone is beyond comprehension. God has gifted us all with an amazing capacity for knowledge. The first thing that God gives us the ability to know is HIMSELF.

Even those with an intellectual disability can have knowledge of God. They may not express it in the same words that we use to write this text, but they, like everyone, have the capacity for knowledge. In fact, someone in this situation would have a knowledge that I will never have. God has gifted all of us with different knowledge for different things.

In the book of Corinthians it likens the body of Christ (God's people) to the human body. The body of Christ has different parts that do different things so that together it makes up the body as a whole.

God will have gifted you with knowledge that is different to the knowledge of others around you. It will not only be academic knowledge, but also the knowledge formed by your life experiences and your own relationship with God.

TODAY'S QUESTION:
Do you consider yourself as a person of knowledge?

TODAY'S ACTION:

Share something of 'your knowledge' with someone else today. Not in the sense of showing off an astute intellect, but pass on a valuable lesson that you know will help someone else.

DAY 38

The sixth Gift of the Holy Spirit is: **Reverence**.

Some people confine reverence to 'being quiet in a Church.' This is part of it, but not at all the extensiveness. In fact, someone could be entirely silent whilst in the Church, but still be entirely irreverent at the same time.

The Hebrew word literally means to "stand in awe, to have a deep respect or honor." He is worthy to be praised, adored, honoured, respected, feared and reverenced.

To have reverence for God is to stand in awe of Him for all that He has done to redeem us.

Through the Gift of Reverence God gives us the ability to encounter Him whilst we engage in these actions.

TODAY'S QUESTION:
How do you show reverence towards God?

TODAY'S ACTION:
In your prayer time today, be especially conscious of the God you are praying to, perhaps kneel or bow your head or find your own way to show a deep sense of honor to Him.

DAY 39

The seventh Gift of the Holy Spirit is: **Wonder and Awe.**

When was the last time that you thought about God and responded with "WOW?"

A quick fix is to walk through the bush, look out of an airplane window, watch a sunset or sit at a river or beach. Reflect for a few minutes on God's creation and you will almost certainly respond with "WOW."

Wonder and Awe is not limited to just marveling at creation. We can look with wonder at things like healings, God's power, and at the journey of one's life.

When we respond to these things by elevating our perspective of God we are indeed using the gift of Wonder and Awe. Doing this puts our life into perspective. It reminds us that we are not really the most powerful being on earth and reminds us that God will always be supreme.

TODAY'S ACTION:
Find something amazing that you can look at for five minutes today. It could be as simple looking up at the stars in the night sky, or looking at the photo album from the time that your child was born. As you look at it, reflect on God until you find yourself saying 'WOW.'

DAY 40

You can probably tell by now that during 'A Season of Renewal' we have looked at different aspects of our Christian life in different blocks of content. After each block I want to make sure that everything is consolidated before we move on and build toward the next thing.

I could summarise what we have looked at so far as:

- How to pray daily

- Incorporating the reading of scripture into our prayer time

- Doing an examination of conscience

- Using the Beatitudes to help with our examination of conscience and our daily life

- Implementing six ways to walk daily with God

- Living out the Gifts of the Holy Spirit in our lives

I stress again that no matter how much content you learn over this 90 days, the thing that will help renew you every single day is having a personal prayer time with God. I want to encourage you to pray for at least fifteen minutes each day. If it hasn't become a habit yet, it may not be long!

TODAY'S QUESTION:

Which section of '90 Days of Renewal' has been most valuable for you so far?

TODAY'S ACTION:

Please send an email to me at 90days@TheCatholic-Guy.com as I would love to hear that you are up to Day 40 and would love to hear what it is that's been most valuable to you so far.

DAY 41

As you know, we recently looked at the Gifts of the Holy Spirit.

In Galatians 5:22-23, the listed Fruits of the Holy Spirit are:

- Love

- Joy

- Peace

- Patience

- Kindness

- Goodness

- Faithfulness

- Gentleness

- Self Control

At times in my life, when I choose against God's will, I stop these things from flowing out of me. I may only stop it on an occasion, or I may block it for a long period of time. Needless to say, I haven't always displayed these nine fruits in their fullness.

Over the next nine days we will give you a chance to reflect daily on a different fruit, providing an opportunity for you to re-examine how you live these things in your life.

TODAY'S QUESTION AND ACTION:

During your personal prayer time, reflect on whether you currently struggle to display any of the nine fruits in your life.

DAY 42

Today we begin reflecting on the Fruits of the Holy Spirit. Today we begin reflecting on the first of the nine Fruits of the Holy Spirit and the first is: **LOVE**.

Love is both an easy one and a hard one to reflect on. It's an easy one because it is something that everyone can relate to in some way or another. It can however be a hard one to relate to because movies and television programs sometimes give us the idea that love is about romance, emotion or feeling. This is of course an element of love, but the scriptural understanding of love is far deeper than this.

We read in 1 John 4:16 (NLT) that **God is love**. The passage continues to say:

> *"all who live in love live in God, and God lives in them. And as we live in God, our love grows more perfect."*

It's clear; if we are a person of LOVE then God will live in us. This in turn helps us to love more!

A few verses later the Bible says:

> *If someone says, "I love God," but hates a fellow believer, that person is a liar; for if we don't love people we can see, how can we love God, whom we cannot see? And he*

*has given us this command: Those who love God must
also love their fellow believers.*

1 John 4:20-21 (NLT)

This tells us that it's not enough to love God and keep it at that. We must show love to people!

TODAY'S QUESTION:

Who are the people that you interact with on a regular basis? In what ways do you show love to them?

TODAY'S ACTION:

Make a list in response to the question above, and then go out of your way to show love in some way to each of these people today.

DAY 43

---

oday we are looking at the second Fruit of the Holy Spirit: **JOY**.

We might think that JOY is a bit cheesy, and all about being chirpy and smiling all day, even a bit superficial. In reality, it's far more than this. Let's look at what the Bible says about **JOY**:

> *"...for the joy of the Lord is your strength."*

> Nehemiah 8:10 (NLT)

Having God in our lives brings joy, which gives us strength.

> *"A merry heart does good, like medicine."*

> Proverbs 17:22 (NKJV)

Being a person of joy is good for our soul.

> *"A man has joy by the answer of his mouth, and a word spoken in due season, how good it is!"*

> Proverbs 15:23 (NKJV)

We know whether we are a person of joy by noticing the things we say. Does it reflect goodness?

TODAY'S QUESTION:

Would others describe you as a person of joy? This is more than just being a nice person. Do you have a sense of joy within you that affects others when they are around you?

TODAY'S ACTION:

Be deliberate to express joy in the words you speak today. During your prayer time reflect on how this has affected your day, and the day of others.

DAY 44

T oday we are looking at the third fruit of the Holy Spirit: **PEACE**.

Peace is the result of resting in a relationship with God. Jesus speaks of peace on the eve of his crucifixion:

> *"I am leaving you with a gift—peace of mind and heart. And the peace I give is a gift the world cannot give. So don't be troubled or afraid."*

John 14:27 (NLT)

Jesus has given us the gift of peace in our lives. It does not mean that trials will not come our way, but it does mean that PEACE can prevail. We know that throughout history many wars have been fought. Conflict is inevitable. Thankfully in many cases peace has eventuated. This is the same in our lives. God has blessed us with peace as a fruit that grows from our relationship with Him.

God doesn't promise that life will be without trial or struggle, but He does give us the gift of peace that we can claim for ourselves in the midst of the ups and downs of life.

TODAY'S QUESTION:
Are there things in your life that seem to bring out the opposite feeling to that of peace?

87

TODAY'S ACTION:

During your personal prayer time today make a list of things that could be causing unrest in your life at the moment. After making this list, pray that God would grant you peace in the midst of these circumstances.

DAY 45

Today we will look at the fourth Fruit of the Holy Spirit: **PATIENCE**.

Patience (and impatience) can exist at a number of levels.

The first context might be when you are standing in a queue and there seems to be very little movement taking place. The person at the counter is going very slowly and you feel a sense of impatience with the situation.

The second context might be when you decide to follow a dream. You might start a business, start renovating a house, or start a charity group. You might even have the sense that God really wants you to do this, and you really hope that straight away you will see amazing change taking place. You soon find that it will be a long journey until your dream is realised.

In both contexts, patience is needed. God knows that we need patience in our lives, this is why He gives this to us through the Holy Spirit!

Let me ask you a timely question: **Do you have any sense of frustration of not feeling 100% renewed as yet from participating in this course?** If you are a little frustrated and life still feels the same as when you started... be patient! Today marks the EXACT HALF WAY point in '90 Days of Renewal.' So much has been said but yet we are only half way... it's the perfect time to be reminded that PATIENCE is important.

TODAY'S QUESTION:

How patient are you in both the little things and the big things?

TODAY'S ACTION:

When you catch yourself about to internally or externally suffer from impatience, say a quick prayer asking the Holy Spirit to grace you with the ability to exercise patience.

DAY 46

Today we will look at the fifth Fruit of the Holy Spirit:
KINDNESS.

Very often someone might define kindness in the same way
that they would define love. Yet they are very clearly listed as two
different Fruits of the Holy Spirit. Kindness is the showing of
sympathy or concern for those in trouble or need. It might be
shown in speech, generous acts, or forgiveness. Yet showing love
sometimes might look like the opposite of kindness. Let me give
you an example.

If I see someone in need on the street and I have some money in
my pocket I will most likely give it to them without asking any
questions, this being described as an act of kindness. On the same
day one of my children might come to me asking for money. I will
probably ask a few questions about what they need it for. If I realise
that they only want to go shopping and that they have already spent
their own weekly wage, then I might decide to withhold giving
them money and instead speak with them about being more re-
sponsible with their spending. This is of course because I love
them and because I know that this will help them more than the
money will.

The challenge for us as Christians is to be able to discern when the
right times are to display kindness. Jesus clearly displayed kindness
on numerous occasions: feeding the crowds, healing the sick and
defending the weak.

I like to think of kindness as the things I do for others not because

I have to, but because I desire to show them the love of God by making something a little easier for them.

TODAY'S QUESTION:

When was the last time that someone showed kindness to you, even if it was something small? How did it make you feel?

TODAY'S ACTION:

The good thing about kindness is that we have endless opportunities to show kindness. I challenge you to show kindness to someone in the next thirty minutes. It doesn't matter where you are or who is around you, there are always ways that we can make something a little easier for another person. Complimenting a shop attendant, making a cup of tea for someone who is tired, doing a task on behalf of someone else... the list goes on.

DAY 47

Yesterday we looked at KINDNESS and today we look at the next Fruit of the Holy Spirit which is: **GOODNESS**.

We often use these words interchangeably, as they are indeed very similar things. The best way to think of goodness is to compare it against the opposite, which is evil.

Jesus said:

> *"The good man brings good things out of the good stored up in him, and the evil man brings evil things out of the evil stored up in him."*

> Matthew 12:35 (NIV)

In this verse Jesus describes the 'good man' as opposite to the 'evil man.' The most insightful thing in this verse is that the 'good man' is not called this just because he does good things. He is called this because he has goodness inside of him. So we learn that genuine goodness is more than the actions, it's a deep presence of goodness in one's life.

This means that a person who appears to be doing 'good things' but really has evil motives and an impure heart is not actually displaying the fruit of 'goodness.'

TODAY'S QUESTION:

When was the last time that you did something good for someone? Why did you do it? Was it a result of genuine goodness within you, or did you maybe have your own agenda?

TODAY'S ACTION:

Throughout this course I have been encouraging you to do a daily examination of conscience. Make sure that you definitely do this today and focus on reflecting deeply on your motives behind the good things that you did.

DAY 48

Today we will look at the seventh Fruit of the Holy Spirit which is: **FAITHFULNESS**.

Faithfulness describes the relationship we have to the things that are important to us and the commitment we uphold to them.

The Bible talks of God's unwavering faithfulness:

> *If we are faithless, he remains faithful, for he cannot disown himself.*

> 2 Timothy 2:13 (NIV)

It's amazing to know that no matter what, God is faithful to us. He created each of us and is within each of us, so therefore it is not in His nature to ever be unfaithful to us. In giving us this Fruit of the Spirit God's desire is that we too would be entirely faithful in our lives. It's more than just God's desire for us, He actually gives us the capacity to achieve this.

If we are truly going to develop a relationship with Jesus, we need to show faithfulness to Him. When I was much younger, I thought this was just about going to Mass and saying my prayers. I soon realised that faithfulness to Jesus was more than this. Being faithful to my family is more than spending an hour a week with them and saying some words to them. To be faithful to my family I need to be with them, talk and listen to them, give to them, be honest with them and always put them before other things.

Since approaching my relationship with Jesus in the same way it has been transformational for me. Sure, there are times that I am unfaithful to God, but it's the desire to live faithfully that God seeks in us.

TODAY'S QUESTION:

What are the things in your life that you seek to be faithful in? (Relationships, commitments, values.)

TODAY'S ACTION:

During your prayer time today, reflect on the things you listed when answering today's question and prayerfully ask God to grace you with faithfulness for these things.

DAY 49

Today we are looking at the eighth Fruit of the Holy Spirit: **GENTLENESS**.

If, like me, you are a man reading this, then don't misunderstand gentleness as being only a feminine characteristic or as a form of weakness. Remember in the days where men were described as 'gentlemen?'

Gentleness is to be humble, tender, aware and to display the actions of Jesus. Nobody would define Jesus as weak, yet everyone would describe Him as gentle. In the Old Testament we read many stories of violence and fighting. Yet when Jesus came to earth He showed us that influence can indeed be far greater with a gentle approach.

Gentleness will express itself in our care and nurture of others. It helps us avoid unnecessary conflict and approach things in a selfless way. This way of interacting gives power to relationships and is beneficial to everyone involved.

Gentleness is not purely a physical characteristic. Have you ever met an older person who appears gentle in appearance, only to later realise that there is a streak of bitterness or aggression within them that is awkward to be around? There is a big difference between the 'grumpy old lady next door' and the 'nice old lady down the street,' yet they often look exactly the same.

TODAY'S QUESTION:

Would you describe yourself as a gentle person? Why, why not?

TODAY'S ACTION:

Make a concerted effort to respond in a gentle nature to any request or comment that is made today.

DAY 50

T oday we are looking at the ninth and final Fruit of the Holy Spirit: **SELF CONTROL**.

Self-control is the translation of the Greek word **enkrateia**, which means: possessing power, strong, having mastery or possession of. Self-control is an action. As much as it suggests being about 'not doing something,' it equally involves 'consciously doing something else'.

The Bible has a famous verse about **self control**:

> *"One who is slow to anger is better than the mighty, and one whose temper is controlled than one who captures a city."*

Proverbs 16:32 (NRSVCE)

I personally feel strongly about how important it is to develop self-control. The reason for this is that self-control is usually needed when emotions are high and the pressure is on. It's virtually impossible to artificially manufacture self-control, which makes it an excellent indicator of the true state of the heart. It is possible to show kindness even without feeling it and it's possible to pretend to be patient whilst being agitated inside. But with self-control, if you are displaying it, then it means you possess it.

People will teach you techniques about self-control, such as taking deep breaths, or counting to ten. This might help in the case of anger, but the breadth of self-control is far greater than this. Self-control requires the development of strong convictions about right and wrong in different situations and being able to overcome the sinful temptations of the flesh and the world. It's even more than convictions; it's about turning them into the action.

Every person requires self-control for different things, but God knows that we need it and has graced us with the ability to live out this fruit in our lives.

TODAY'S QUESTION:

What are the areas of your life that you particularly struggle with self-control?

TODAY'S ACTION:

Stop right now and pray a ten-second prayer asking God to give you the grace to show self-control for one of the areas you listed when answering the above question. For the rest of the day, as often as you are tempted, stop and pray the same prayer.

DAY 51

O ver the last nine days we have focussed on the nine Fruits of the Holy Spirit. Hopefully you learnt a few new things along the way but it's important to remember that they are meant to be far more than just nine things to learn about.

As you work on displaying the nine Fruits of the Holy Spirit then they should become something that others notice about your life. They are far more than 'self-improvement' tips, as it requires God's grace for us to be able to display them fully.

Take this opportunity to look back through the nine fruits. It will be normal to realise that with some of them you have made little progress. This reminds us that we need God's grace again and again to develop these fruits in us.

TODAY'S QUESTION:
Which fruits of the Holy Spirit have you found the most challenging to display?

TODAY'S ACTION:
In relation to the answer you wrote for the question above, turn back a few pages and look back at the 'Today's Action' that followed the notes of these particular fruits. Make these actions your actions for today.

DAY 52

A couple of times through this course I have used the term 'relationship with God.' You may be very familiar with this phrase, you may have read it without thinking anything at all, or you may have stopped and thought what it really means.

The term 'relationship with God' is both a reality and a challenge. The truth is that God desires a relationship with every single person. We know that God created us in His image and likeness (Genesis 1:26) but the connection between us and God doesn't stop there. We read that God's thoughts about us are innumerable (Psalm 139:17) and continuous.

The best way of describing how God wants to connect with us is using the term 'relationship.' The reason I described this as being a challenge is because I know that a relationship is a responsibility. I can't leave everything about my spiritual life over to God. If it truly is to be a relationship then I need to put in time, effort and sacrifice. But at the same time, I can expect the wonders and blessings that come from a healthy relationship.

Like any relationship, it takes time to develop. The more time I spend in prayer and seeking after God the more I can genuinely describe my interaction with God as a relationship. I would encourage you to see this as being possible for your life too... it's definitely God's desire.

TODAY'S QUESTION:

Do you consider your current connection with God as a 'relationship?'

TODAY'S ACTION:

Look back at Day 30 where we listed the six ways to 'Walk Daily With God.' These things are the things that help us develop a 'relationship' with God. Remind yourself of these and practice as many as you can today.

DAY 53

———————— ◢ ————————

In the early part of this course I encouraged you to read through a short passage of the Bible every day. I suggested a simple method based mainly on reading and reflecting on the passage afterward.

Over the next four days I will teach you a simple method of studying Bible passages that I was taught many years ago. It is known as the S.O.A.P method and I have taught this to thousands of people who have found it very helpful.

The **S** in the acronym stands for **Scripture**.

This involves selecting a passage of scripture for you to study. As you get started, I suggest choosing a heading in the Gospel books (New Testament) that stands out to you. Take time reading and allow God to speak to you. Then read it a second time and highlight, underline or place a mark in the margin of your Bible next to the parts that stand out. When you are done, reread the verses you marked looking for something that stands out to you and write it in your journal.

Some people don't like writing in a Bible but I have found it can be very helpful. I know it's a sacred book and deserves respect, but I also know that God has given it to us so that we can study it, digest it and get the most out of it. Church buildings are sacred places too but we understandably put up signs for exits and bathrooms, notice boards, lights and attach boxes to the walls for newsletters or mission collections. All of these things are the practical things that are added to the sacred place so that it works on a practical level.

This is the reason I am not afraid to make notes in my Bible, I know it will help me on a practical level.

TODAY'S QUESTION AND ACTION:
Find a passage of the Bible and begin to study it using the instructions from this session. When you do this, what is it that stands out to you from the passage?

DAY 54

In yesterday's session we started on the S.O.A.P method for studying the Bible. In the question and action from yesterday you chose a passage of the Bible to use, which you will need to have ready again to use with this session and the remainder of the S.O.A.P method session.

The **S** in the acronym stands for **Scripture**.

The **O** in the acronym stands for **Observe**.

By reflecting on the part that stands out at you from the passage, consider what God might be saying to you in this scripture. Ask the Holy Spirit to teach you. Even if Jesus is not mentioned in the passage, what do you think He would say to you if He wanted to teach you something from this passage? It might help to paraphrase the passage in your own words in your journal.

TODAY'S QUESTION AND ACTION:
Using the same passage as yesterday, expand on the study using the instructions from this session. What do you observe that God might be saying to you through the passage?

DAY 55

We are now halfway through learning the S.O.A.P method for studying the Bible. Our goal in using this method is that we would be able to let the verses of the Bible come alive and be real in our lives right now.

The **S** in the acronym stands for **Scripture**.

The **O** in the acronym stands for **Observe**.

The **A** in the acronym stands for **Application**.

In the APPLICATION step you should personalise what you have read by asking yourself how it applies to your life right now. Perhaps it is instruction, encouragement, revelation of a new promise or corrections for a particular area of your life. Write how you feel you can live this passage in a practical way today.

TODAY'S QUESTION AND ACTION:
Using the same passage again, expand on the study using the instructions from this session. What is the practical application for your life?

DAY 56

We are now ready to look at the final step in using the S.O.A.P method to study the Bible.

The **S** in the acronym stands for **Scripture**.

The **O** in the acronym stands for **Observe**.

The **A** in the acronym stands for **Application**.

The **P** in the acronym stands for **Prayer**.

The S.O.A. that we have focused on so far are very practical steps. The final step of PRAYER reminds us that the Bible is more than just practical tips but is the living word of God. The prayer at the end of your S.O.A.P. study can be as simple as asking God to help you use this scripture, or it may be a greater insight on what He may be revealing to you. Remember, prayer is a two-way conversation, so be sure to listen to what God has to say and write it in your journal.

TODAY'S ACTION:
Using the same passage again, expand on the study using the final instructions for prayer that were suggested in this session.

DAY 57

My hope and prayer is that in the last four days you were able to engage deeply with God by using the simple S.O.A.P. method of studying the Bible. I aim to do this for a different chapter of scripture every day of my life and it has been transformational for me.

Like doing anything new, there are a few things you should be aware of so that you don't start interpreting the Bible in the wrong way.

Remember these things:

1. **Be especially attentive to the content and unity of the whole scripture.** Avoid focusing too much on a single verse. Rather, look at content of the whole chapter (or book) in which it was placed.

2. **Be attentive to the analogy of faith.** This means looking at the coherence of the truths of the Bible and ensuring what we draw from one place is backed up in another.

TODAY'S QUESTION:
How have you benefitted from the S.O.A.P. method in the past four days? What parts have been most difficult?

TODAY'S ACTION:

Instead of doing the S.O.A.P. steps over four days, set aside some time to do the whole process in one sitting, using a new passage of scripture.

DAY 58

W hilst doing the S.O.A.P. Bible study, and at other times in this course, I have often asked a question like "what is God saying to you?"

The idea of God speaking to us is far more than just analysing our thoughts and reflections. We believe that through **THE HOLY SPIRIT** we actually do experience God's presence. In the next few sessions we will deepen our understanding and appreciation of the Holy Spirit, an important part of the Holy Trinity.

The Spirit has spoken through the prophets and helps us hear God through the Bible, but we do not hear the Spirit Himself.

The various places where we see the Holy Spirit alive are:

- In the scriptures, the word of God

- In prayer

- In our spirits

- Through the church

- In our giftings

- In our circumstances

TODAY'S QUESTION:

Which things in the list above match up with times that you have previously stopped and appreciated that the Holy Spirit is alive and present? Are there some in which you never really acknowledged the role of the Holy Spirit?

TODAY'S ACTION:

Choose one thing from the list above that you can engage in today. As you engage in it, be deliberate about encountering the Holy Spirit and focus on being fully aware of God's presence.

DAY 59

In yesterday's session we looked at the Holy Spirit and the means in which the Holy Spirit is present.

The term 'Spirit' translates the Hebrew word ruah, which, in its primary sense, means breath, air, wind. Jesus indeed uses the sensory image of the wind to suggest to Nicodemus the transcendent newness of himself.

Today we will look at the many images and symbols of the Holy Spirit:

- **Water** signifies the Holy Spirit's action in Baptism

- **Fire** symbolises the transforming energy of the Holy Spirit

- **Cloud and Light** describes many encounters in the Bible that people had with God

- **The Seal** indicates the indelible effect of the Holy Spirit

- **The hand** represents the Holy Spirit present in the laying on of hands during prayer

- **The finger** was used when Jesus cast out demons and when God's law was written on stone

- **The dove** appeared at the end of the flood and symbolises peace with God

TODAY'S QUESTION:

Which of the above symbols of the Holy Spirit do you easily or readily identify with? Why?

TODAY'S ACTION:

Choose one symbol from the list above that you didn't automatically find familiar and reflect on the description of that symbol. Throughout the day keep reminding yourself of that aspect of the Holy Spirit. You might benefit from finding an image or item that represents that symbol so that you can place it in a prominent place today as a reminder.

DAY 60

I n the past two sessions we have looked at the places and symbols of the Holy Spirit, but today we will remind ourselves that **the best way to understand the Holy Spirit is to understand Jesus.** As part of the trinity the person of Jesus and the presence of the Holy Spirit are inseparable.

This means that it is by the anointing of the Spirit that Jesus had power. How then could WE expect to have power without the anointing of the Spirit? As we live the life that Jesus modeled for us, we will be claiming the anointing of the Holy Spirit in our own lives.

Logically and scientifically the Holy Spirit is a hard concept to process. I don't pretend to know everything about the working of the Spirit. In fact, I am comforted that Mary was confused by how the Spirit could impregnate her, but yet she could still go on to live a life that has eternal influence. There is hope for all of us yet, even if we don't understand everything!

TODAY'S QUESTION:
Are you comfortable knowing that some aspects of the Holy Spirit are difficult to grasp or understand?

TODAY'S ACTION:
During your personal prayer time today make a deliberate effort to move beyond the motions and routine of prayer and experience the power of the Holy Spirit that is present.

DAY 61

My hope in this whole 90-day journey is that you would grow closer to Jesus and experience amazing richness in your faith. It would be difficult for me to lead you through 90 days and not focus briefly on Mary, the mother of Jesus. Mary knows better than anyone what it means to be devoted to Jesus and what it means to sacrifice so much for the will of God.

So what is Mary's role now?

Mary has always been a central figure in Christianity. She's always been absolutely key, right from that moment early in Luke's gospel when she's told, "Blessed are you amongst women."

The significance of Mary's life was not based on any of the things our world values so highly—background, physical beauty, intelligence, education, natural gifts, and abilities. It was Mary's relationship to Jesus that gave her life significance. "*The Lord is with you,*" the angel told her (Luke 1:28, NIV). That is what made all the difference in this young woman's life. And it is what makes all the difference in our lives.

In her life I have found a wealth of wisdom for my own walk with God.

TODAY'S QUESTION:
Would you say that Mary has played a role in your own faith journey? Why/why not?

TODAY'S ACTION:

Read Luke 1:26-38 and do a S.O.A.P study on this passage to see what the scriptures reveal to you today through your focus on Mary.

DAY 62

W ords do have an important part to play in our personal relationship with God even though there is nothing we can say to God that He doesn't already know.

When we tell someone that we love them, it is an important statement for both the person who says it and the person who is the recipient of our declaration of love.

With God, when we tell Him that we love Him, it does not change Him for He is unchangeable. God has always loved us and always will. Our admission of love and desire to be in a personal relationship with God changes us. When we tell God the desires of our heart, make our requests known to Him and express in words our praise, worship and adoration of Him, something happens in us. We are changed.

TODAY'S QUESTION:
Do you find it difficult to declare your love for the people in your life, for God? Why or why not?

TODAY'S ACTION:
During your prayer time declare and write words that express your love for God. If this is difficult, sit quietly and say it simply.

DAY 63

I n today's session I want to encourage you to do a little assess-
ment and revision as to how your daily personal prayer time is
going. It would be fairly easy to push your prayer time into the
background because you are already spending a few minutes each
day to work through this 90-day course.

I really want to make it clear. The daily readings in this course won't
bring about renewal in your life just by reading them. The renewal
and transformation come when you put everything into action and
focus diligently on prayer, lifestyle and disciplines using the information in these sessions as a guide and prompt.

My personal prayer time each day is something I have to work hard
to protect. I have to protect it from my busy life. I have to protect
it from others who require my time, and I have to protect it from
my own thoughts and attitudes that sometimes try and place other
things as a higher priority.

If you find that your personal prayer time is wavering a little
remember the many things that I focused on earlier in this course:

- Pray in a suitable and consistent place

- Use a journal and write out your prayers

- Pray like you are having a normal conversation
  with God

- Reflect on what God might be saying to you through

the thoughts and experiences you are having

- Do a daily examination of conscience going through the beatitudes and gifts and fruits of the Holy Spirit

- Use the S.O.A.P method to study a passage of scripture

- Aim to pray for at least fifteen minutes each day

TODAY'S QUESTION:
Which of the suggestions in the list above have you been able to sustain and which have been difficult for you?

TODAY'S ACTION:
When you pray today make a deliberate effort to incorporate all of the suggestions in the list.

DAY 64

O ne of the amazing things about the way God created mankind is that He has given us the gift of freedom. I once heard someone describe God as the 'absolute gentlemen who never forces anything on anyone.'

Of course, God has the power to make mankind believe in Him, but then this would not be a relationship of love. The Bible says:

> *It was he who created humankind in the beginning,*
> *and he left them in the power of their own free choice.*

Sirach 15:14 (NRSVCE)

By giving us freedom we shape our own life and can seek the creator in our own way, and attain perfection when we are directed towards God.

My exposure to the Catholic church was through my upbringing in a Catholic family but for a while my involvement was really only because of tradition, culture, respect and routine. In my teenage years I was challenged by a priest to exercise my own free will and make my own decision about my faith. I have encouraged thousands of people to make their own decision in the past and I encourage you to think about it today.

TODAY'S QUESTION:

Has there been a point in your life when your relationship with God was weaker than it is now? What changed for you to decide to strengthen it?

TODAY'S ACTION:

Make the decision again! Whether it be the decision for a relationship with God or a decision to inquire further, exercise the free will to decide, which God has given you.

DAY 65

Yesterday I talked about man's freedom and I would like to expand on this today. The great thing about the freedom God gives us is that it's continuous. Not only do we have freedom of choice when it comes to our response to Jesus' invitation, we have freedom of choice every moment of every day.

There are a few things to keep in mind when it comes to using our freedom the way God intended:

> **SIN:** With this freedom comes the consequence of sin. From the outset of mankind sin has been a reality. Our challenge is to use our freedom to choose against sin and not give in to this inclination, knowing that from time to time, sin is imminent.

> **GRACE:** It is not God's desire that we make the free decision to sin because of the grace that is assured to us.

> **RIGHTS:** The right to freedom does not mean that we have a right to say or do everything. We should always consider the moral law and not use our freedom in ignorance of the rights of others.

The gift of freedom is just like a precious gift that you might receive from a loved one. We usually take great care of something that is valuable, especially if it is something priceless, like a family heirloom. The gift of freedom can be approached in a similar way. We should always be aware of it and ensure that we don't abuse or neglect such a wonderful gift.

TODAY'S QUESTION:

Do you consciously consider the will of God in the decisions that you make?

TODAY'S ACTION:

Be intentional about every decision you make today. As you make each decision, stop and ask yourself whether you are choosing for or against God's will.

DAY 66

In the coming sessions we will look at the 'virtues' of the faith. **A virtue is a habitual and firm disposition to do good.**

Our human and moral virtues are the attitudes and habits that we have that cause us to respond in a particular way. For example, if my children get angry towards me and I manage to respond in a positive and sensitive way then it could be said that my 'good' response is a result of my human virtue.

The first of these is: **PRUDENCE.**

St Thomas Aquinas said: "Prudence is right reason in action." It is prudence that immediately guides the judgment of conscience. A prudent person is one who determines and directs their conduct in accordance with this judgment. It is seen by having rule and measure in our responses.

This is such a valuable virtue because it means that as we apply our principles to things that arise we will avoid the possible result of error or indeed evil.

TODAY'S QUESTION:
Would you describe yourself as someone who possesses the virtue of prudence?

TODAY'S ACTION:

After making a simple decision of some kind today, stop and reflect on whether you feel you possessed prudence when making that decision.

DAY 67

The second virtue, which we will look at in this session, is: **JUSTICE**.

Justice is the virtue that leads a person to give toward both God and their neighbour. A person who displays this virtue seeks the common good.

Remember that we are talking about a virtue, which is something internal. It's one thing to make automatic payments to sponsor a child (which is a great thing) but to do this out of virtue and not out of pressure, guilt, fashion or habit is a totally different thing. When a person makes this kind of decision because of a firm will and a strong conviction then it could be said that they have the virtue of justice.

The scriptures refer often to the 'just man' as the person who always has genuine care and concern in their conduct toward their neighbour. We all know people who could be described like this, and I'm sure you'll agree that these people are inspirational.

 TODAY'S QUESTION:
Would you describe yourself as someone who possesses the virtue of justice?

TODAY'S ACTION:

It can't be switched on automatically, but do your best to do something for the goodwill of others today, something that moves you.

DAY 68

I n recent days we have looked at the first two cardinal virtues of prudence and justice. The third virtue is: **FORTITUDE**.

Fortitude is the virtue that ensures firmness in difficulty and adversity. Not only does it help us 'do good' in these situations but it helps us resist temptations, conquer fears and endure persecution.

There is a great verse in the Bible that describes fortitude:

> *"In the world you will have tribulation; but be of good cheer, I have overcome the world."*

John 16:33 (NKJV)

We all suffer 'bumps in the road' throughout our life. Sometimes this could arise within family, career, hopes and dreams, or in a variety of relationships. For this reason the virtue of fortitude is relevant to us all. This verse from John says that in these times we should be of 'good cheer.' I don't know about you but in these times it's often hard to just feel peaceful, let alone of 'good cheer.' However, it is very encouraging to know that God has made it possible for us to be so hopeful despite tribulations.

TODAY'S QUESTION:
Would you describe yourself as someone who possesses the virtue of fortitude?

TODAY'S ACTION:
During a difficulty today, say a quick prayer asking God to develop the virtue of fortitude in you so that you can be of 'good cheer.'

DAY 69

The fourth virtue which we will look at in this session is: **TEMPERANCE.**

In everyday language we commonly use the word 'temper,' to describe the expression or response that someone might react with. The context of temperance as a virtue includes this but it is also far broader. As a virtue, temperance is what balances the attraction of all kinds of pleasures and ensures our mastery over instincts. It also helps us keep desires within the limits of what is honourable.

In the Bible it says:

> *"Do not follow your inclination and strength, in pursuing the desires of your heart."*

Sirach 5:2 (NRSVCE)

It is so easy to go with our human inclinations and desires in so many situations. It's easy to say words we don't really mean or eat food that we know is bad for us. On a larger scale there are plenty of ways that we could respond to situations that could lead to significant pain, guilt and hardship for both others and self. God is well aware that we all suffer from temptation and therefore desires to help us all develop the virtue of temperance.

TODAY'S QUESTION:
Would you describe yourself as someone who possesses the virtue of temperance?

TODAY'S ACTION:
When you are about to respond to a situation today, stop for a moment and seek to filter your response through the virtue of temperance.

DAY 70

The virtues help us relate directly to God and help us participate in a relationship with the Father, Son and Holy Spirit.

In this session we will look at the virtue: **FAITH**.

In seems very strange to be writing about 'faith' so far into this course. It seems so elementary because this whole course is written on the pretext that you are already aware of the concept of faith. My desire, however, is to be able to reflect on all of the virtues, so I don't want to miss this one out.

Put simply, faith is the virtue by which we believe in God and believe all that He has said and revealed to us. The virtue of faith is more than just a 'belief.' To live out this virtue we must keep the faith, live it daily, profess it, confidently bear witness to it, and spread it. This is the part of faith that many people find most challenging.

TODAY'S QUESTION:
How well are you doing at displaying the fullness of this virtue? Is your faith private to you or do you live it out in the way it was described above?

TODAY'S ACTION:
Look for an opportunity during the day to profess, bear witness, or spread your faith.

DAY 71

I n this session we will look at the virtue of: **HOPE.**

Hope is the virtue in which we desire the kingdom of heaven and the eternal life. In hope we place our trust in Christ's promises rather than in our own strength.

Every person I know desires happiness in their life. Regardless of whether they are Christian, of another faith, or haven't made a faith decision of any kind, everyone I know has aspirations for happiness. In fact, we believe that God has placed this aspiration inside all people. For Christians and Catholics, the virtue of hope is our response to this desire.

The virtue of hope is more than belief. It is what aids us during discouragement, sustains us during abandonment, and opens our heart in expectation of the eternal life.

In the Bible we read of how Abraham possessed great hope. In Genesis 17:4-8, Abraham displays great hope as he takes up his duty of fulfilling the hope of the entire Chosen People. In Genesis 22:1-19, Abraham was preparing to even sacrifice his son because of the hope he had in God's promises. I wonder whether we hope in God's promises to the level that Abraham did? He was definitely blessed as a result!

TODAY'S QUESTION:

Would you say that you have the virtue of hope? Remember that this is different from faith.

TODAY'S ACTION:

Choose something that you hope for from your relationship with God. It could be a particular healing, provision, miracle, or something that you long for. Write this down and put it somewhere where you will notice it constantly throughout the day. Every time you see this, be sure to access the virtue of hope within you, rather than just an acknowledgment of the words.

DAY 72

———————✦———————

The final of all virtues we will look at in this course is: **CHARITY.**

Charity is the virtue by which we love God. Genuine charity involves us loving God not for our own sake, but for His sake. Because of our love for God, true charity extends to loving our neighbour. The 'love of neighbour' is the context in which we might be more familiar with the term charity. Many good 'charities' provide for the needs of disadvantaged people, but the root of this virtue is love for God which leads to our love for people.

There is a famous passage of the Bible in which the Apostle Paul focuses on charity:

> *"charity is patient and kind, charity is not jealous or boastful; it is not arrogant or rude. Charity does not insist on its own way; it is not irritable or resentful; it does not rejoice at wrong, but rejoices in the right. Charity bears all things, believes all things, hopes all things, endures all things."*

1 Corinthians 13:4-7 (CCC)

You might be more familiar with the translation of this passage in which the word 'love' replaces 'charity.' Regardless, of the reasons for this in different translations, it tells us that the two things are very similar.

TODAY'S QUESTION:

Would you say that you have a 'love' of God that exists regardless of what grace, blessing or satisfaction you might get out of the relationship?

TODAY'S ACTION:

We know that God wants us to 'ask' for things, but in your prayer time today spend a little more time expressing your love for God, rather than asking for blessing.

DAY 73

In the past seven sessions we looked at seven Christian virtues. We will use this session to look back at these.

St Gregory of Nyssa said: *"The goal of a virtuous life is to become like God."*

I find this a wonderful quote. We know that we have been created in the image and likeness of God, yet sometimes it's easy to feel like our life doesn't reflect this. By developing and displaying the virtues we have looked at we now have some specific and focused things that will help mould us more into God's likeness.

This also reminds us that the virtues are not supposed to be a checklist that we need to attain in order to have achieved something in life. They are a guide to one thing, being more like God.

 ## TODAY'S QUESTION:
Which of the seven virtues do you find most challenging? Why do you think that this is the case for you?

 ## TODAY'S ACTION:
Using the virtue that you answered in the question above, place a special focus on developing and displaying this today.

DAY 74

I n this course I have talked a lot about prayer. It is has been irreplaceable for me in my own relationship with Jesus.

You may have wondered why I haven't yet referred to 'The Lord's Prayer' which is often also referred to as the 'Our Father.' The reason for this is two-fold. Firstly, I didn't want anyone doing this course to assume that this was the only way to pray. Secondly, because I wholly believe in its importance I wanted to dedicate a number of sessions to The Lord's Prayer and I feel that this stage of the course is the best place to do so.

You will probably be very familiar with this prayer. It is found in Matthew 6:9-13 as well as Luke 11:2-4. In case you are new to the faith, here is the prayer as it is commonly said:

Our Father who art in heaven,

hallowed be thy name.

Thy kingdom come,

Thy will be done

on earth as it is in heaven.

Give us this day our daily bread,

and forgive us our trespasses,

as we forgive those who trespass against us,

and lead us not into temptation,

but deliver us from evil.

The reason it is called The Lord's Prayer is that Jesus suggests that empty phrases and impressive words and are much better replaced by praying this prayer.

TODAY'S QUESTION:

What role has saying The Lord's Prayer played in your individual prayer life?

TODAY'S ACTION:

Pray The Lord's Prayer slowly and deliberately, reflecting on every word.

DAY 75

Yesterday I introduced that a number of sessions would be dedicated to understanding The Lord's Prayer. Commencing in this session we will look at it line by line, as it is a prayer of incredible substance.

It is not my intention that we would talk about each line from an academic perspective but rather that you would gain an understanding of how each line can connect you closer to Jesus.

It may seem obvious, but the first line is *Our Father*.

You will notice that it is not 'my' Father. For this reason it has become known as the Prayer of the Church. The 'our' reminds us that God does not belong to me individually in a possessive sense. He is also the Father of our Lord Jesus Christ, and He will last well beyond my earthly life.

By acknowledging God as Father as we commence the prayer, we are humbling ourselves before God. We are placing God in a position of authority and power over us, much as the imagery of an earthly father might suggest. In our quest to know and be like Jesus we are acknowledging that we need the Father.

TODAY'S QUESTION:
In the past have you humbled yourself before God as you commenced praying?

TODAY'S ACTION:
Spend some time at the start of your personal prayer time today to elevate your perspective of God.

DAY 76

A s we work through the lines of The Lord's Prayer we will spend this session to focus on *who art in heaven*.

This expression is not referring to a physical place or space. Instead, it refers to a way of being. From the time we are young it is suggested to us that God lives in heaven which is 'up in the clouds.' In order to understand this line we must push aside these pre-conceived ideas.

God is indeed in heaven, but it is much closer than in a northerly universe and even closer than the clouds above us. In fact, Our Father is not even "elsewhere." So, where is He? God is transcendent of everything, God is in the hearts of people, and in the Church. In His majesty God is present everywhere!

There is a well-known story of a teacher who asks her six-year-old student what she is drawing on the page. The student responds that she is drawing 'heaven.' The teacher says, "but nobody knows what heaven looks like." In their innocence the child replies, "they will when I'm finished."

TODAY'S QUESTION:
What is your picture of heaven?

TODAY'S ACTION:

Back on Day 26 of this course I introduced you to the concept of having 'constant conversation' with God. To remind you that God is ever present today, place a special focus on constant conversation.

DAY 77

B y praying "Our Father, who art in heaven" we have placed ourselves in the presence of God to love and bless Him. The lines that follow are known as the SEVEN PETITIONS. The first three draw us toward the glory of God and the last four describe our need for His grace.

The first petition, and the line of The Lord's Prayer that we will look at today is **hallowed be thy name.**

'Hallowed' refers to being holy. Not in the sense that we make God holy in this prayer, because only God makes things holy, but in the sense that we acknowledge the divine and holy nature of God. Holy refers to being 'set apart.' You might refer to a wonderful Christian person as being a 'holy person' because they are set apart from what is normal. You might also refer to a church building as a holy place, because it is unique and set apart from normal buildings.
But none of these things are as holy as God, as they are made Holy by God.

TODAY'S QUESTION AND ACTION:
During your prayer time, prayerfully reflect on all of the things that makes God set apart from us. Make a list of these. (e.g. miracles, creation, perfect, etc)

DAY 78

The next petition, and the line of The Lord's Prayer that we will look at today is ***thy kingdom come***.

This refers primarily to the final coming of the reign of God through the return of Jesus, referred to commonly as the 'end times.' This of course could be a long way off, as it has been about 2000 years of waiting so far.

We should not be too distracted by the distant future because this line encourages us also to commit strongly to our mission in the present times. It is God's plan that we would experience the 'kingdom' here on earth.

> *"The Kingdom of God is...righteousness and peace and joy in the Holy Spirit."*
>
> Romans 14:17 (NKJV)

The Holy Spirit is with us so it is indeed possible for us to experience the blessings of the kingdom whilst here in our earthly lives.

TODAY'S QUESTION:
Do you believe that your own personal world is becoming more like heaven or going in another direction?

TODAY'S ACTION:

Be deliberate today to take one thing away from your own world that would not fit peacefully within God's kingdom. It could be reading a gossip magazine, being involved in negative humour, or anything that is often part of normal life, but not the kingdom.

DAY 79

The next petition, and the line of The Lord's Prayer that we will look at today is ***thy will be done on earth as it is in heaven***.

In the Bible it talks about God's desire to see all people changed whilst on earth:

> *"God our saviour, who desires everyone to be saved and to come to the knowledge of the truth."*

1 Timothy 2:3-4 (NRSVCE)

God is not just the God of the heavens but also the God of the earth. God's will for us on earth is endless.

Keep in mind that we are radically incapable of living fully according to God's will, but through Jesus and the Spirit we can surrender our own will to Him. This is the first and most important step in living God's will.

By looking at the scriptures we can learn some key ways to live in God's will whilst we are on earth:

1. **Love one another** (2 Peter 3:8) This is the greatest of all commandments and summarises all of the others.

2. **Obtain the inheritance of Jesus** (Ephesians 1:9-11) Through our relationship with Jesus we are able to move towards God's loving plan which already exists in heaven.

3. **Live in a way that pleases God** (John 8:29) We do this

through the habits and disciplines that we have covered in this whole course.

TODAY'S QUESTION:

Have you fully surrendered your own will to God, and asked God for His will?

TODAY'S ACTION:

During your personal prayer time today, put today's question into action, even if you have done it many times before.

DAY 80

The next petition, and the line of The Lord's Prayer that we will look at today is ***give us this day our daily bread***.

The words 'give us' remind us that we are reliant on the provision of God. It also expresses the commitment we make to God and the commitment God makes to us. We are His and He is ours. Our daily bread encompasses the many things that we need. St Cyprian said: *"Since everything indeed belongs to God, he who possesses God wants for nothing."*

For those who genuinely suffer from a lack of bread and food, this petition has a profound meaning. Because it says give 'us,' this petition is indeed a cry from the whole Church for God to bless others in the human family that are in desperate need.

TODAY'S QUESTION:
What is the daily bread that you most desire? What is it that you picture when you are asking God to bless you?

TODAY'S ACTION:
Spend a moment praying for something that you are seeking from God, but then also pray for the bread that others are seeking.

DAY 81

The next petition, and the line of The Lord's Prayer that we will look at today is ***and forgive us our trespasses, as we forgive those who trespass against us.***

We all need forgiveness. I know I do. According to these words, our petition for forgiveness will not be heard unless we have first met the strict requirement of offering forgiveness to others.

It also says that as God is forgiving us we are forgiving others, reminding us that we are made in God's image and reflect His love and forgiveness to the world.

In this petition we are like the prodigal son, who goes before his father with a confession and a request for his mercy. The great thing is that God's mercy is assured to all who come to Him. Colossians 1:14 tells us that in Jesus we find redemption and the forgiveness of sins.

It's so important that we aren't complacent even though God pours His mercy in abundance. If we have not forgiven those who have trespassed against us, then God's mercy, though present, will not penetrate our hearts.

I started by saying that we all need forgiveness, and we do. But we all need to give forgiveness as well.

TODAY'S QUESTION:
What is something that you need to be forgiven for?
Also, is there anyone you need to forgive?

TODAY'S ACTION:
This could be a big one. Pick up the phone and call someone that you haven't spoken with for a long time because of a conflict or disagreement. Don't try and engage the conflict, just speak with them from the perspective of a person who has forgiven them.

DAY 82

T he next petition, and the line of The Lord's Prayer that we will look at today is *and lead us not into temptation*.

I always found this an interesting line of The Lord's Prayer, as I couldn't imagine that God the Father would lead us into temptation (it says this in James 1:13). The reality is, what we are asking God is not to allow us to take the path that leads to sin.

God is not going to impose good onto us. He is going to offer it, but He wants us to be free in our choices. Our inner being grows when we discern the ways of God for ourselves. Whilst temptation is dangerous, there is a certain usefulness to it. Imagine that you have two teenage children. One of them has been offered drugs by their friends and they refused it. Your other teenager has never been offered drugs at all. We couldn't say which of them is 'better off' but we could say that the one who has proven that they can choose against this temptation has developed and demonstrated an amazing quality.

> *"God is faithful, and he will not let you be tested beyond your strength, but with testing he will also provide the way out so that you may be able to endure it."*

1 Corinthians 10:13 (NRSVCE)

This scripture verse clarifies that we can ask God to lead us out from any point of temptation. God is not against us being tempted. The question then becomes; if God provides a way out, will you take it?

TODAY'S QUESTION:

In what areas of life do you suffer from temptation?

TODAY'S ACTION:

We all sin daily, so when you see yourself at the point of temptation (no matter how big or small) be deliberate today to choose God's way out.

DAY 83

The next petition, and the line of The Lord's Prayer that we will look at today is ***but deliver us from evil.***

We haven't referred to 'evil' much in this course, but it is very much a reality of our lives. Hollywood often pictures evil as some kind of dramatic abstraction, but in the case of Christianity, evil is a person. Evil is Satan, the devil, the angel who opposes God. Evil tries to throw himself across God's plan. Because of Evil sin entered the world.

I don't want to make it dramatic, but it would be safe to say that we have all been affected by the Evil One at some point in our lives. Sometimes our mistakes are a result of our own stupidity, but there may have been times when you listened to the voice of the Evil One, disguised in some way. Because we can all relate to this, this final part of The Lord's Prayer is relevant to everyone.

When we pray this petition we ask for two things. Firstly, we asked to be delivered from the voice of the Evil One that is trying to corrupt us at this very moment. Secondly, we are asking to be freed from all evils, past, present and future, of which the Evil One is the author.

TODAY'S QUESTION:
Are you familiar with the idea that the Evil One is present in our everyday world?

TODAY'S ACTION:

As you go about the day, have an awareness that the Evil One may wish to tempt you away from the things of God today.

DAY 84

In recent sessions we have looked line by line at The Lord's Prayer. I am convicted that since Jesus gave us this prayer, then He definitely wants us to understand it. Imagine the transformational effect that this prayer could have if, between you and God, you were able to bring to life everything that the prayer encompasses?

It is communal in vocabulary, but don't let this stray you into thinking it only belongs in the congregation.

My challenge to you is to pray this as part of your daily personal prayer time—not for the sake of saying the words, but for the sake of humbling yourself, worshipping God and asking for the things of God.

 TODAY'S QUESTION:
How has your perspective on The Lord's Prayer changed since working through these recent sessions?

 TODAY'S ACTION:
Put simply, pray it. Pray it like you've never prayed it before.

DAY 85

We are now inside the last week of what I hope and pray has been an amazing time of renewal in your faith. As we come towards the end, these remaining sessions are focused entirely on things that will help you walk the long journey of faith in your life.

One of the strongest suggestions I give to people who are serious about their faith is to find another person who can act as a mentor or faith partner with you. I call this person a GROW PAL. Not only does 'pal' refer to a friend or buddy, but it forms the acronym P.A.L. which stands for three valuable ways that this person can help you 'grow.'

The **P** in the acronym stands for **POWER**.

Your Grow Pal should be someone that empowers you. They should be someone who can encourage you in your faith and in the goals that you have. They should also give you the power to be vulnerable with them so that you can share struggles and difficulties with them. They don't have to be your best friend, and you don't have to really know them at all, but you should feel a sense of peace knowing that they are walking your journey with you. This is much like the way a battery provides the power for a device.

In the next two sessions we will look at the other two components that a Grow Pal should offer.

TODAY'S QUESTION:

Have you had someone in your life that has played the role of a Grow Pal before, even if you haven't referred to them as this?

TODAY'S ACTION:

Say a prayer that over the coming days God will reveal someone to you that will be a valuable Grow Pal to you.

DAY 86

Yesterday we commenced looking at the importance of having a Grow Pal. In addition to providing 'power' the Grow Pal should offer **ACCOUNTABILITY**.

If we are going to change any habits or disciplines in our life then accountability is important. This would involve your Grow Pal asking you the questions that relate to the areas of change that you are trying to achieve in your life. You probably have things in your life that you want to stop doing or do differently, and your Grow Pal can ask you regularly how successful you have been in this goal. In a similar way you might want to start doing something, or start doing something better, like praying every day or reading the Bible every day. Your Grow Pal can constantly question you and remind you.

In our busy lives it's hard to frequently spend time with a Grow Pal so they might be able to offer accountability by giving you a phone call or sending you an SMS or email.

TODAY'S QUESTION AND ACTION:
In what areas of your life would you benefit from having accountability? Make a list of these ready for when you choose a Grow Pal.

DAY 87

In the past two days we have covered the first two things that a Grow Pal should offer you.

P stands for **POWER**

A stands for **ACCOUNTABILITY**

And in this session, we will look at **L** which stands for **LOVE**

There are two kinds of love that this person should be able to provide for you. The first of these I call 'soft love.' This is our most common picture of love and might involve them consoling you when things are tough, and reassuring you when you are doubtful.

The second kind of love I call 'tough love.' This is the kind of love that nobody likes but we all need. It's the kind of love I show my kids when they are disobedient in some way which might result in some kind of punishment. I only do this because I love them. You want your Grow Pal to love you enough so that they will be real and 'beat you up' (metaphorically) when you are ignorant or blind to something that they can see but you can't.

Overall, you want your Grow Pal to be committed to you growing in your faith.

TODAY'S QUESTION:

Now that you are familiar with the role of a Grow Pal, who is someone that you could ask to be a Grow Pal to you?

TODAY'S ACTION:

Be bold and brave and ask this person today to be your Grow Pal. (You might need to tell them all about what a Grow Pal is!)

DAY 88

A number of times in the past 90 days we have referred to having a personal relationship with Jesus. This is what Jesus desires for us and in my experience it is the irreplaceable ingredient for renewal.

I don't want you to get to the end of this course and have gained only knowledge. The knowledge won't bring fulfillment and the knowledge will probably fade away. But if you can be convicted in your desire to have a relationship with Jesus then you will gain far more in your life after this course than anything you might have gained or experienced whilst doing it.

At times in my life I have developed my experience of different things, and it usually involves establishing a relationship with someone who is accomplished in that area. I developed my interest in birds by establishing a relationship with a bird club, and I developed my interest in cycling by developing a relationship with a cyclist. It goes without saying that the single most important way to develop your faith is to develop a relationship with Jesus.

Remember your relationship with Jesus is developed primarily through prayer. Throughout this course we have looked extensively at prayer and if necessary, go back through the pages that will help you with this.

TODAY'S QUESTION AND ACTION:

Sit down with your journal and write as much as you can to describe the type of relationship with Jesus that you desire to have.

DAY 89

In this, the second to last session of a long journey, I would like to make you aware of a responsibility that you have. It might sound like a speech that a sports coach gives their team in the last scene of a sports movie, but it is deeply rooted in Christianity.

This responsibility is to do more than 'be good.' The responsibility is to be voluntary and generous in the way we engage with society. We need to 'promote good.' There are certain ways that we can do this, including taking care in educating your family, being conscientious in your work, and taking an active part in community life. I hope that this course has made you a better person, but I would be delighted if you could go out into the world and make the world a better place.

In all of my years of ministry I have been exposed increasingly to a world that has a real need for people to participate. Your attendance, service, creativity and witness are needed as much now as they've ever been. This is a great opportunity for you and me, as we have a genuine opportunity to see our contribution make a visible difference.

TODAY'S QUESTION:
In what ways would you say that you currently participate?

TODAY'S ACTION:
Commence doing something today that increases the level in which you 'participate.'

DAY 90

Congratulations on making it to the end of this 90-day journey. In this last session it is not my intention to summarise, but I do want to remind you of the key things that I hope you have learned from this course.

- God's will is for us to be in relationship with Him

- Our relationship with God is built through prayer

- Prayer should be a part of our daily life

- One way to pray is as though we are having a normal a conversation with God using a journal

- Reflect in prayer on what God might be saying to you through your thoughts and experiences

- Incorporate a prayer such as The Lord's Prayer

- Do a daily examination of conscience going through the beatitudes and gifts and fruits of the Spirit

- Use the S.O.A.P method to study a passage of scripture each day

- Our lifestyle should involve walking daily with God whilst displaying the human and moral virtues

- Find a Grow Pal

Finally, I should point out that renewal will not peak in 90 days. Renewal is a daily occurrence and should be an ongoing part of your life. This course has given you many of the tools, now you have a lifetime to try and implement them all!

TODAY'S QUESTION:

In what ways have you experienced renewal as a result of this 90-day course?

TODAY'S ACTION:

Send me an email at 90days@TheCatholicGuy.com as I would love to hear that you have finished this '90 Days of Renewal.'